ICONS

MEXICO STYLE

MEXICO

Exteriors   Interiors

STYLE

Details

EDITOR **Angelika Taschen**

PHOTOS **Barbara & René Stoeltie**

TASCHEN

KÖLN LONDON LOS ANGELES MADRID PARIS TOKYO

Front cover: Looking in: Salvador Reyes Rios' kitchen, Mérida
Couverture: Vue de l'intérieur: la cuisine de Salvador Reyes Rios, Mérida
Umschlagvorderseite: Ausblicke: Die Küche von Salvador Reyes Rios, Mérida

Back cover: Looking out: Patio seating at Salvador Reyes Rios' house
Dos de couverture: Vue de l'extérieur : le coin-repos dans le patio de Salvador Reyes Rios
Umschlagrückseite: Einblicke: Die Sitzecke im Patio von Salvador Reyes Rios

Also available from TASCHEN:

Living in Mexico
200 pages
3–8228–2890–4 (English/French/German)
3–8228–2891–2 (edition with French cover)

To stay informed about upcoming TASCHEN titles, please request our magazine
at www.taschen.com or write to TASCHEN, Hohenzollernring 53, D-50672 Cologne,
Germany, Fax: +49-221-254919. We will be happy to send you a free copy
of our magazine which is filled with information about all of our books.

© 2005 TASCHEN GmbH
Hohenzollernring 53, D-50672 Köln
www.taschen.com

Concept by Angelika Taschen, Berlin
Layout and general project management by Stephanie Bischoff, Cologne
Texts by Christiane Reiter, Berlin
Lithography by Horst Neuzner, Cologne
English translation by Pauline Cumbers, Frankfurt am Main
French translation by Thérèse Chatelain-Südkamp, Cologne

Printed in Italy
ISBN 3–8228–4014–9

CONTENTS SOMMAIRE INHALT

The house looked as if the blue of its walls had poured down directly from the sky, as if the sun had covered the door and window frames with yellow kisses, and as if the canopy had been tickled by the bougainvillea until it was literally pink. Entering the rooms you found yourself treading on kiwi-green carpets, sitting on pink sofas, and gazing at turquoise walls in front of which strelizia in vases seemed to emit flaming orange lightning flashes. Anywhere else people would reach for their sunglasses to withstand such a surge of stimuli – in Mexico, such colours amount to a celebration. Mexico is an architectural and artistic empire unfamiliar with black-and-white painting. Even early high cultures such as that of the Maya produced glistening gold ornaments and mosaics of coloured feathers; the Spanish colonial masters constructed their buildings using vibrant volcanic rock or limestone and were liberal with colours when having them painted; and later the representatives of Muralismo told the history of their country in radiant murals.

LAND OF COLOUR
Christiane Reiter

En regardant la maison, on avait l'impression que le bleu du ciel avait éclaboussé ses murs, que le soleil avait laissé un baiser jaune sur le cadre des portes et des fenêtres et que le bougain-villée avait chatouillé l'avant-toit jusqu'à ce que celui-ci en rou-gisse. A l'intérieur, on marchait sur des tapis couleur kiwi, on s'asseyait sur des canapés rose bonbon et on voyait des murs bleu turquoise devant lesquels les oiseaux de paradis dans leurs vases dessinaient des éclairs orangés. Partout ailleurs le visiteur aurait chaussé aussitôt ses lunettes de soleil pour supporter une telle agression de son nerf optique – au Mexique toutefois ces couleurs étaient une véritable fête pour l'œil. Le Mexique est un pays qui ignore le noir et blanc aussi bien dans son architecture que dans sa culture. Des civilisations très développées, comme celle des Mayas, fabriquaient déjà des bijoux en or étincelants et des mosaïques de plumes multicolores, les colonisateurs espa-gnols érigeaient leurs bâtiments avec des pierres calcaires ou des pierres de volcan colorées et puisaient largement dans leur boîte à couleurs pour les badigeonner, et plus tard, les repré-sentants du Muralismo racontèrent l'histoire de leur pays sur des

Das Haus sah aus, als sei das Blau auf seinen Mauern direkt vom Himmel geflossen, als hätte die Sonne Tür- und Fensterrahmen gelb geküsst, und als wäre das Vordach so lange von der Bougainvillea gekitzelt worden, bis es vor Lachen über und über errötete. Wer die Zimmer betrat, lief über kiwigrüne Teppiche, saß auf pinkfarbenen Sofas und blickte auf türkise Wände, vor denen Strelizien wie orangeflammende Blitze in Vasen standen. Überall sonst hätten Besucher sofort zur Sonnenbrille gegriffen, um einer solchen Reizüberflutung Herr zu werden – in Mexiko jedoch waren diese Farben ein Fest. Mexiko ist ein Reich, das auf architektonischem und künstlerischem Gebiet keine Schwarz-Weiß-Malerei kennt. Schon Hochkulturen wie die Maya stellten glänzenden Goldschmuck her und Mosaike aus bunten Federn, die spanischen Kolonialherren ließen mit farbigem Vulkan- oder Kalkstein bauen und griffen beim Tünchen tief in den Malkasten, und später erzählten die Vertreter des Muralismo auf leuchten-den Wandbildern von der Geschichte ihres Landes. Auch beim Stil-mix waren der Fantasie niemals Grenzen gesetzt: Indianisch inspirierte Kacheln, maurische Torbögen, üppige Barockfassaden

When it came to mixing styles, there were no limits to the imagination: Indian-inspired tiles, Moorish arches, opulent Baroque facades, or Neo-classicist forms – in Mexico these are all possible, ideally in one and the same building. This may sound like creative chaos, but on closer inspection a common denominator can be discovered: "An attentive eye will notice that a certain continuity exists despite the difference in the works and epochs," Octavio Paz once wrote, "not the continuity of a style or an idea, but something much deeper and less easily explicable: sensibility." The delight which Mexicans take in colours and patterns can also be discovered in the pictures of this book – taken in simple Maya houses and former haciendas, in converted monasteries and chapels, and in private villas on the Pacific in which designers have realised their dreams. Travel with us to the Land of Colour, experience outdoor and indoor worlds in all the colours of the rainbow – and leave your sunglasses at home.

fresques éclatantes. Même en mélangeant les styles, les Mexicains ne furent jamais à court d'imagination : carreaux d'inspiration indienne, arcades mauresques, opulentes façades baroques ou formes néoclassiques – au Mexique, on trouve de tout dans un seul et même bâtiment et ce, d'une façon idéale. On pourrait penser que ce mélange a un côté fouillis créatif, mais celui qui se donne la peine d'observer tout cela d'un peu plus près, trouvera un dénominateur commun. « Un œil attentif remarquera qu'il existe bien une certaine continuité dans cette variété d'œuvres et d'époques », écrit un jour Octavio Paz, « non pas la continuité d'un style ou d'une idée, mais quelque chose de beaucoup plus profond et de moins explicable : la sensibilité. » C'est cette sensibilité mexicaine pour les couleurs et les formes que montrent les photos de ce livre, des photos prises dans de simples maisons mayas et d'anciennes haciendas, dans des monastères et des chapelles, ainsi que dans des villas privées de la côte du Pacifique, avec lesquelles les designers ont réalisé leur rêve. Voyagez dans ce pays des couleurs, savourez ces mondes intérieurs et extérieurs dans tous les tons de l'arc-en-ciel, et surtout laissez vos lunettes de soleil dans leur étui.

oder neoklassizistische Formen – in Mexiko gibt es alles und idealerweise alles im selben Gebäude. Das klingt ein bisschen nach kreativem Chaos; aber wer genauer hinsieht, findet einen gemeinsamen Nenner: „Ein aufmerksames Auge wird merken, dass in der Verschiedenheit der Werke und Epochen doch eine gewisse Kontinuität besteht.", schrieb Octavio Paz einmal, „Nicht die Kontinuität eines Stils oder einer Idee, sondern etwas viel Tieferes und weniger Erklärbares: Sensibilität." Das Gespür, das man in Mexiko für Farben und Muster besitzt, zeigen auch die Bilder dieses Buches – aufgenommen in einfachen Mayahäusern und ehemaligen Haciendas genau so wie in umgebauten Klöstern und Kapellen und Privatvillen am Pazifik, mit denen sich Designer ihren Traum verwirklicht haben. Reisen Sie mit ins Land der Farben, erleben Sie Außen- und Innenwelten in allen Nuancen des Regenbogens – und lassen Sie Ihre Sonnenbrille zu Hause.

"… A restless nature exuding the aroma of bougainvillea and verbena, of freshly cut pineapple and bleeding melon …"

Carlos Fuentes, in *The years with Laura Diaz*

« … C'était une nature agitée qui embaumait les bougainvillées et la verveine, l'ananas fraîchement coupé et les melons mûrs … »

Carlos Fuentes, dans *Les Années avec Laura Díaz*

» … Es war eine ruhelose Natur, die nach Bougainvilleen und Eisenkraut, nach frisch zerschnittener Ananas und blutender Melone duftete … «

Carlos Fuentes, in *Die Jahre mit Laura Díaz*

EXTERIORS

Extérieurs Aussichten

70/71 At two levels: life at Villa Mi Ojo, Costa Careyes. *Sur deux étages : habiter dans la Villa Mi Ojo, Costa Careyes.* Auf zwei Etagen: Wohnen in der Villa Mi Ojo, Costa Careyes.

72/73 Blue-and-white stripes: open air salon at Tigre del Mar, Costa Careyes. *Rayures bleues et blanches : dans le salon en plein air de Tigre del Mar, Costa Careyes.* Blau-weiß gestreift: Im Freiluftsalon von Tigre del Mar, Costa Careyes.

74/75 Filigree decor: Salvador Reyes Rios' kitchen, Mérida. *Décoration filigrane : la cuisine de Salvador Reyes Rios, Mérida.* Filigran verziert: Die Küche von Salvador Reyes Rios, Mérida.

76/77 Geometry: floor mosaic in the lobby of Tigre del Mar, Costa Careyes. *Géométrie : sol en mosaïque dans l'entrée de Tigre del Mar, Costa Careyes.* Geometrie: Fußbodenmosaik in der Lobby von Tigre del Mar, Costa Careyes.

78/79 19th century: bedroom furniture in Hacienda Poxila, Mérida. *Datant du XIXe siècle : meubles dans la chambre de l'hacienda Poxila, Mérida.* Aus dem 19. Jahrhundert: Möbel im Schlafzimmer der Hacienda Poxila, Mérida.

80/81 Relaxing: seats at Hacienda Petac, Yucatán. *Invitation à la détente : sièges dans l'hacienda Petac, Yucatán.* Zum Zurücklehnen: Sitzgruppe in der Hacienda Petac, Yucatán.

82/83 Cheerful colours: sofas in the rotunda of Sol de Oriente, Costa Careyes. *Couleurs gaies : canapés dans la rotonde de Sol de Oriente, Costa Careyes.* Fröhliche Farben: Sofas in der Rotunde von Sol de Oriente, Costa Careyes.

84/85 Wood with patina: the dining room at Hacienda Petac, Yucatán. *Bois avec patine : dans la salle à manger de l'hacienda Petac, Yucatán.* Holz mit Patina: Im Esszimmer der Hacienda Petac, Yucatán.

86/87 Imaginative lamp: in the salon at Hacienda Xcumpich, Mérida. *Lustre plein d'imagination : dans le salon de l'hacienda Xcumpich, Mérida.* Fantasievoller Leuchter: Im Salon der Hacienda Xcumpich, Mérida.

88/89 Bright yellow tiles: bathroom at Museo Robert Brady, Cuernavaca. *Carreaux couleur de soleil : salle de bains du Museo Robert Brady, Cuernavaca.* Sonnengelbe Kacheln: Bad des Museo Robert Brady, Cuernavaca.

90/91 All the colours of the rainbow: fabrics in Casi Casa, Costa Careyes. *Dans tous les tons de l'arc-en-ciel : étoffes dans la Casi Casa, Costa Careyes.* In allen Farben des Regenbogens: Stoffe in der Casi Casa, Costa Careyes.

92/93 Sweet dreams: guestroom at Casi Casa. *Doux rêves : dans la chambre d'ami de la Casi Casa.* Süße Träume: Im Gästezimmer der Casi Casa.

94/95 Pink frame: bull's eye at Casitas de las Flores, Costa Careyes. *Cadre rose : œil de bœuf dans les Casitas de las Flores, Costa Careyes.* Rosa Rahmen: Bullauge in den Casitas de las Flores, Costa Careyes.

96/97 Homage to the Orient: bedroom at the Museo Robert Brady, Cuernavaca. *Hommage à l'Orient : chambre au Museo Robert Brady, Cuernavaca.* Hommage an den Orient: Schlafzimmer im Museo Robert Brady, Cuernavaca.

98/99 Like a mask: vaulted room at Museo Robert Brady. *Une multitude de masques : salle voûtée au Museo Robert Brady.* Maskenhaft: Gewölbesaal im Museo Robert Brady.

100/101 The wheel of history: at the Hacienda Petac, Yucatán. *La roue de l'Histoire : dans l'hacienda Petac, Yucatán.* Das Rad der Geschichte: In der Hacienda Petac, Yucatán.

102/103 Long table: Victor Manuel Contreras' salon, Cuernavaca. *Longue table : dans le salon de Victor Manuel Contreras, Cuernavaca.* Lange Tafel: Im Salon von Victor Manuel Contreras, Cuernavaca.

104/105 Effective: the landing in Victor Manuel Contreras' house. *Fait de l'effet : le palier dans la maison de Victor Manuel Contreras.* Wirkungsvoll: Der Treppenabsatz im Haus von Victor Manuel Contreras.

106/107 Rustic: living room under blue wooden beams. *Rustique : la salle de séjour sous les poutres peintes en bleu.* Rustikal: Wohnzimmer unter blau gestrichenen Holzbalken.

108/109 Antiquities galore: at the house of John Powell and Josh Ramos, Mérida. *Intérieur équipé d'objets anciens : chez John Powell et Josh Ramos, Mérida.* Mit Antiquitäten ausgestattet: Bei John Powell und Josh Ramos, Mérida.

110/111 Natural emphasis: at the house of John Powell and Josh Ramos. *Accents naturels : dans la maison de John Powell et Josh Ramos.* Natürliche Akzente: Im Haus von John Powell und Josh Ramos.

112/113 Simply beautiful: Medici-style vase of John Powell and Josh Ramos. *Un bijou sobre : vase dans le style Médicis chez John Powell et Josh Ramos.* Schlichtes Schmuckstück: Vase im Medici-Stil bei John Powell und Josh Ramos.

114/115 Clear forms and gentle tones: Salvador Reyes Rios' living room, Mérida. *Formes claires et couleurs douces : dans la salle de séjour de Salvador Reyes Rios, Mérida.* Klare Formen und sanfte Töne: Im Wohnzimmer von Salvador Reyes Rios, Mérida.

116/117 Chill out: resting area in the bedroom of Mi Ojo, Costa Careyes. *Chill out : relaxation dans la chambre de Mi Ojo, Costa Careyes.* Chill out: Ruhebereich im Schlafzimmer von Mi Ojo, Costa Careyes.

118/119 All in white: another bedroom at Mi Ojo's. *Tout en blanc : une autre chambre de Mi Ojo.* Ganz in Weiß: Ein weiteres Schlafzimmer von Mi Ojo.

"… Torches were burning on the gallery pillars sending out glowing sparks and radiating the aroma of Ocote pine resin …"

Rosario Castellanos, in *The Book of Lamentations*

«… Aux piliers de la galerie brûlaient avec ardeur des flambeaux qui jetaient des étincelles et répandaient le parfum de la résine de pin …»

Rosario Castellanos, dans *Oficio de tinieblas*

»… An den Säulen der Galerie brannten heftig lodernd funkensprühende Fackeln, die den Duft nach dem Harz der Ocotekiefer verströmten …«

Rosario Castellanos, in *Das dunkle Lächeln der Catalina Díaz*

CHARMING DETAILS

Détails charmants Charmante Details

126 Radiant colours: at Casi Casa, Costa Careyes. *Couleurs éclatantes : dans la Casi Casa, Costa Careyes.* Farben mit Leuchtkraft: In der Casi Casa, Costa Careyes.

128 Fiery red: strelizia at Hacienda Petac, Yucatán. *Rouge vif : oiseau de paradis dans l'hacienda Petac, Yucatán.* Feuerrot: Strelizie in der Hacienda Petac, Yucatán.

129 A touch of Antiquity: bronze sculpture at Victor Manuel Contreras' home. *Souvenir de l'Antiquité : bronze chez Victor Manuel Contreras.* Andenken an die Antike: Bronzeskulptur bei Victor Manuel Contreras.

130 Marble: bath tub at Hacienda Petac, Yucatán. *En marbre : baignoire dans l'hacienda Petac, Yucatán.* Aus Marmor: Badewanne in der Hacienda Petac, Yucatán.

132 Facial features: masks in Sol de Oriente, Costa Careyes. *Rictus : masques dans la maison Sol de Oriente, Costa Careyes.* Gesichtszüge: Masken im Haus Sol de Oriente, Costa Careyes.

133 Red and round: staircase at Sol de Oriente. *Rouge et ronde : la cage d'escalier de Sol de Oriente.* Rot und rund: Treppenhaus von Sol de Oriente.

134 The colour of the sun: ironing room at Hacienda Xcumpich, Mérida. *La couleur du soleil : pièce de repassage dans l'hacienda Xcumpich, Mérida.* Die Farbe der Sonne: Bügelzimmer in der Hacienda Xcumpich, Mérida.

136 Vitamin C: a dish of limes. *Vitamine C : une coupe de limettes.* Vitamin C: Eine Schale mit Limetten.

137 All in yellow: parrot room at Hacienda Xcumpich, Mérida. *Tout en jaune : la chambre au perroquet dans l'hacienda Xcumpich, Mérida.* Ganz in Gelb: Papageienzimmer in der Hacienda Xcumpich, Mérida.

138 Sunny times: mural at the home of Sarah Sloan. *Ensoleillée : peinture murale chez Sarah Sloan.* Sonnige Zeiten: Wandmalerei bei Sarah Sloan.

140 Enticing: siren relief at Casa dos Estrellas, Costa Careyes. *Ensorcelant : relief de sirènes dans la Casa dos Estrellas, Costa Careyes.* Verlockend: Sirenen-Relief in der Casa dos Estrellas, Costa Careyes.

141 Blue frame: painted tiles at the home of Sarah Sloan. *Cadre bleu : carreaux peints chez Sarah Sloan.* Blauer Rahmen: Bemalte Fliesen bei Sarah Sloan.

142 In the corner: yellow throne at the home of Sarah Sloan. *Au coin : trône jaune chez Sarah Sloan.* In der Ecke: Gelber Thron bei Sarah Sloan.

144 Enamelled: metal basin at Hacienda Xcumpich, Mérida. *Emaillé : évier en fer dans l'hacienda Xcumpich, Mérida.* Emailliert: Eisenbecken in der Hacienda Xcumpich, Mérida.

145 Bird-like: white mask at Hacienda Xcumpich. *Comme un oiseau : masque blanc dans l'hacienda Xcumpich.* Vogelartig: Weiße Maske in der Hacienda Xcumpich.

146 Colours and forms: at Casitas de las Flores, Costa Careyes. *Couleurs et formes : dans les Casitas de las Flores, Costa Careyes.* Farben und Formen: In den Casitas de las Flores, Costa Careyes.

148 Beautiful silhouette: strelizia at Salvador Reyes Rios', Mérida. *Belle silhouette : oiseau de paradis chez Salvador Reyes Rios, Mérida.* Schöne Silhouette: Strelizie bei Salvador Reyes Rios, Mérida.

149 Rolled up: hammock at Salvador Reyes Rios'. *Enroulé : hamac chez Salvador Reyes Rios.* Aufgerollt: Hängematte bei Salvador Reyes Rios.

150 Divine support: the chapel of Hacienda Petac, Yucatán. *Assistance divine : la chapelle de l'hacienda Petac, Yucatán.* Göttlicher Beistand: Die Kapelle der Hacienda Petac, Yucatán.

152 Soaring: ladder at Tigre del Mar, Costa Careyes. *S'élance vers le ciel : échelle à Tigre del Mar, Costa Careyes.* Aufstrebend: Leiter in Tigre del Mar, Costa Careyes.

153 Bizarre: stone artwork at Mi Ojo, Costa Careyes. *Bizarre : œuvre d'art en pierre à Mi Ojo, Costa Careyes.* Skurril: Steinernes Kunstwerk in Mi Ojo, Costa Careyes.

154 Sky blue: stairs at Tigre del Mar, Costa Careyes. *De la couleur du ciel : escalier à Tigre del Mar, Costa Careyes.* In der Farbe des Himmels: Treppe in Tigre del Mar, Costa Careyes.

156 Shady: on the veranda at Mi Ojo, Costa Careyes. *Bandes d'ombre : sur la véranda de Mi Ojo, Costa Careyes.* Schattenstreifen: Auf der Veranda von Mi Ojo, Costa Careyes.

157 From blue to green: look-out at Mi Ojo. *Du bleu au vert : petite ouverture à Mi Ojo.* Vom Blauen ins Grüne: Kleiner Ausguck in Mi Ojo.

158 Elegance: curved mirror in Hacienda Petac, Yucatán. *Jolies courbes : miroir dans l'hacienda Petac, Yucatán.* Schön geschwungen: Spiegel in der Hacienda Petac, Yucatán.

160 Going up: stairs in Tigre del Mar, Costa Careyes. *En route vers le haut : escalier à Tigre del Mar, Costa Careyes.* Auf dem Weg nach oben: Treppe in Tigre del Mar, Costa Careyes.

161 Going down: the stairwell in Tigre del Mar. *En route vers le bas : toujours dans la cage d'escalier de Tigre del Mar.* Auf dem Weg nach unten: Ebenfalls im Treppenhaus von Tigre del Mar.

162 Symbolic figure: a Calavera Catrina in Casi Casa, Costa Careyes. *Figure symbolique : une Calavera Catrina dans la Casi Casa, Costa Careyes.* Symbolfigur: Eine Calavera Catrina in der Casi Casa, Costa Careyes.

164 Naïve art: small sculpture in Casi Casa. *Art naïf : petite sculpture dans la Casi Casa.* Naïve Kunst: Kleine Skulptur in der Casi Casa.

165 Covered in pearls: mask from the region around Oaxaca. *Brodé de perles : masque de la région d'Oaxaca.* Mit Perlen bestickt: Maske aus der Region um Oaxaca.

166 At the bar: in Casitas de las Flores, Costa Careyes. *Au bar : dans les Casitas de las Flores, Costa Careyes.* An der Bar: In den Casitas de las Flores, Costa Careyes.

168 Singing mermaid: at the Casi Casa, Costa Careyes. *Sirène chantante : dans la Casi Casa, Costa Careyes.* Singende Meerjungfrau: In der Casi Casa, Costa Careyes.

169 The door to happiness: at Casi Casa. *La porte vers le bonheur : dans la Casi Casa.* Die Tür zum Glück: In der Casi Casa.

170 Enticing: chaise longue at Casi Casa. *Invite à s'y étendre : chaise longue dans la Casi Casa.* Zum Hineinlegen schön: Chaiselongue in der Casi Casa.

172 Decorative: door handle at the house of Sarah Sloan. *A motif : poignée de porte dans la maison de Sarah Sloan.* Gemustert: Türgriff im Haus von Sarah Sloan.

173 Colourful accessories: also at the home of Sarah Sloan. *Accessoires colorés : également chez Sarah Sloan.* Bunte Accessoires: Ebenfalls bei Sarah Sloan.

174 Delightful: detail from a painting by Ray Smith. *Invitation au baiser : détail d'un tableau de Ray Smith.* Zum Küssen: Detail aus einem Gemälde von Ray Smith.

176 Golden cage: well-preserved frescoes at Sergio Berger's, Mexico City. *Cage dorée : fresques bien conservées chez Sergio Berger, Mexico.* Goldener Käfig: Gut erhaltene Fresken bei Sergio Berger, Mexiko-Stadt.

177 Favourite spot for a siesta: divan at Hacienda San José, Cacalchen. *Une place idéale pour la sieste : le divan dans l'hacienda San José, Cacalchen.* Lieblingsplatz für die Siesta: Diwan in der Hacienda San José, Cacalchen.

178 Lightly veiled: four-poster bed at Hacienda San José. *Joliment voilé : lit à baldaquin dans l'hacienda San José.* Zart verhüllt: Himmelbett in der Hacienda San José.

180 Stone and plaster: shower cabin at the home of John Powell and Josh Ramos. *Pierre et stuc : cabine de douche chez John Powell et Josh Ramos.* Stein und Stuck: Duschkabine bei John Powell und Josh Ramos.

181 Cornice: silent stone figure at the Museo Robert Brady, Cuernavaca. *Gardien impassible : figure de pierre au Museo Robert Brady, Cuernavaca.* Stummer Wächter: Steinfigur im Museo Robert Brady, Cuernavaca.

182 Traditional construction: car port of Josefina Espejo's palapa house, Mérida. *Construction traditionnelle : abri de voiture de la maison Palapa de Josefina Espejo, Mérida.* Traditionelle Bauweise: Carport des Palapahauses von Josefina Espejo, Mérida.

184 Trio: decorative tassels at Sergio Berger's, Mexico City. *Trio : ravissantes cordelettes chez Sergio Berger, Mexico.* Trio: Schmuckvolle Kordeln bei Sergio Berger, Mexiko-Stadt.

185 Steadfast: statue at Sergio Berger's. *Inébranlable : statue chez Sergio Berger.* Standhaft: Statue bei Sergio Berger.

186 Sweet snacks: fruit-seller on the Yucatán. *En-cas sucrés : vendeur de fruits sur la presqu'île du Yucatán.* Süße Snacks: Obstverkäufer auf der Halbinsel Yucatán.

Addresses

COSTA CAREYES
Gian Franco Brignone
Km 53.5 Carretera Barra de Navidad to Puerto Vallarta, Jalisco
Mexico
Tel. (+52) 315 351 0240
E-mail: info@careyes.com.mx
Website: www.careyes.com.mx

MUSEO ROBERT BRADY
Calle Netzahualcoyotl #4
Cuernavaca, Morelos 62000
Mexico
Tel. (+52) 777 318 8554
E-mail: museobrady@podigy.net.mx

HACIENDA PETAC
Domicilio Petac
Mérida, Yucatán
Mexico
Tel. (+52) 999 910 4334
E-mail: info@haciendapetac.com
Website: www.haciendapetac.com

HACIENDA SAN JOSÉ
Km 30 Carretera, Tixkokob-Tekanto
Tixkokob, Yucatán 97470
Mexico
Tel. (+52) 999 910 4617
E-mail: Reservations1@Grupoplan.com
Website: www.starwood.com

The Hotel Book. Great Escapes Africa Shelley-Maree Cassidy / Ed. Angelika Taschen / Hardcover, 400 pp. / € 29.99 / $ 39.99 / £ 19.99 / ¥ 5.900

The Hotel Book. Great Escapes Asia Christiane Reiter / Ed. Angelika Taschen / Hardcover, 400 pp. / € 29.99 / $ 39.99 / £ 19.99 / ¥ 5.900

The Hotel Book. Great Escapes Europe Shelley-Maree Cassidy / Ed. Angelika Taschen / Hardcover, 400 pp. / € 29.99 / $ 39.99 / £ 19.99 / ¥ 5.900

"This is one for the coffee table, providing more than enough material for a good drool. Gorgeousness between the cover." —*Time Out*, London, on *Great Escapes Africa*

"Buy them all and add some pleasure to your life."

African Style
Ed. Angelika Taschen

Alchemy & Mysticism
Alexander Roob

All-American Ads 40ˢ
Ed. Jim Heimann

All-American Ads 50ˢ
Ed. Jim Heimann

All-American Ads 60ˢ
Ed. Jim Heimann

American Indian
Dr. Sonja Schierle

Angels
Gilles Néret

Architecture Now!
Ed. Philip Jodidio

Art Now
Eds. Burkhard Riemschneider, Uta Grosenick

Atget's Paris
Ed. Hans Christian Adam

Berlin Style
Ed. Angelika Taschen

Cars of the 50s
Ed. Jim Heimann, Tony Thacker

Cars of the 60s
Ed. Jim Heimann, Tony Thacker

Cars of the 70s
Ed. Jim Heimann, Tony Thacker

Chairs
Charlotte & Peter Fiell

Christmas
Ed. Jim Heimann, Steven Heller

Classic Rock Covers
Ed. Michael Ochs

Design Handbook
Charlotte & Peter Fiell

Design of the 20ᵗʰ Century
Charlotte & Peter Fiell

Design for the 21ˢᵗ Century
Charlotte & Peter Fiell

Devils
Gilles Néret

Digital Beauties
Ed. Julius Wiedemann

Robert Doisneau
Ed. Jean-Claude Gautrand

East German Design
Ralf Ulrich / Photos: Ernst Hedler

Egypt Style
Ed. Angelika Taschen

Encyclopaedia Anatomica
Ed. Museo La Specola Florence

M.C. Escher

Fashion
Ed. The Kyoto Costume Institute

Fashion Now!
Ed. Terry Jones, Susie Rushton

Fruit
Ed. George Brookshaw, Uta Pellgrü-Gagel

HR Giger
HR Giger

Grand Tour
Harry Seidler

Graphic Design
Eds. Charlotte & Peter Fiell

Greece Style
Ed. Angelika Taschen

Halloween
Ed. Jim Heimann, Steven Heller

Havana Style
Ed. Angelika Taschen

Homo Art
Gilles Néret

Hot Rods
Ed. Coco Shinomiya, Tony Thacker

Hula
Ed. Jim Heimann

Indian Style
Ed. Angelika Taschen

India Bazaar
Samantha Harrison, Bari Kumar

Industrial Design
Charlotte & Peter Fiell

Japanese Beauties
Ed. Alex Gross

Krazy Kids' Food
Eds. Steve Roden, Dan Goodsell

Las Vegas
Ed. Jim Heimann, W. R. Wilkerson III

London Style
Ed. Angelika Taschen

Mexicana
Ed. Jim Heimann

Mexico Style
Ed. Angelika Taschen

Morocco Style
Ed. Angelika Taschen

New York Style
Ed. Angelika Taschen

Paris Style
Ed. Angelika Taschen

Penguin
Frans Lanting

20ᵗʰ Century Photography
Museum Ludwig Cologne

Photo Icons I
Hans-Michael Koetzle

Photo Icons II
Hans-Michael Koetzle

Pierre et Gilles
Eric Troncy

Provence Style
Ed. Angelika Taschen

Robots & Spaceships
Ed. Teruhisa Kitahara

Safari Style
Ed. Angelika Taschen

Seaside Style
Ed. Angelika Taschen

Albertus Seba. Butterflies
Irmgard Müsch

Albertus Seba. Shells & Corals
Irmgard Müsch

Signs
Ed. Julius Wiedeman

South African Style
Ed. Angelika Taschen

Starck
Philippe Starck

Surfing
Ed. Jim Heimann

Sweden Style
Ed. Angelika Taschen

Sydney Style
Ed. Angelika Taschen

Tattoos
Ed. Henk Schiffmacher

Tiffany
Jacob Baal-Teshuva

Tiki Style
Sven Kirsten

Tuscany Style
Ed. Angelika Taschen

Valentines
Ed. Jim Heimann, Steven Heller

Web Design: Best Studios
Ed. Julius Wiedemann

Web Design: Flash Sites
Ed. Julius Wiedemann

Web Design: Portfolios
Ed. Julius Wiedemann

Women Artists in the 20ᵗʰ and 21ˢᵗ Century
Ed. Uta Grosenick